THE
HOME FRONT

IMAGES OF
WAR

THE
HOME FRONT

Maureen Hill

Photographs by the

Daily Mail

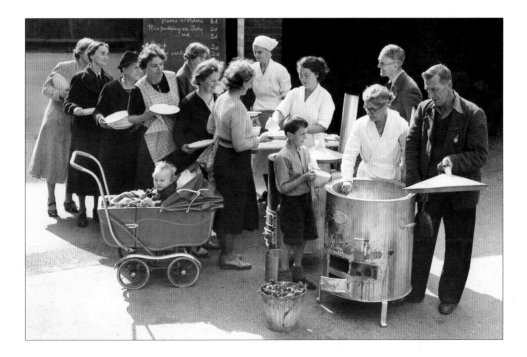

p

This is a Parragon book
This edition published in 2005

Parragon
Queen Street House
4 Queen Street
Bath BA1 1HE

Photographs ©Associated Newspapers Ltd

Text © Parragon 2003

Produced by Atlantic Publishing

A catalogue record for this book is available
from the British Library.

ISBN 1-40544-989-6
Printed in China

Introduction

Fighting the war on the domestic front

'As from eleven o'clock this morning, Britain is at war with Germany.' Neville Chamberlain's words, broadcast on radio on the third of September 1939, confirmed what many people had feared for days and some had seen as inevitable for months. War preparations had been building throughout the year. A Conscription Bill had been introduced in March; Civil Defence plans had been drawn up and at the end of August the evacuation of the vulnerable from the major population centres had begun. As Chamberlain made his announcement, what was unappreciated by everyone was how long the conflict would last, and the degree to which the mass of the British population would be required to fight their own battles to win the war.

Life for everyone in the country soon became one of unremitting toil. The demands of the war were everything. Men, women, children, the young and the old, all had to make a contribution to the 'war effort'. Virtually all manufacturing industry was given over to producing equipment for the war; almost nothing was produced for home consumption – if something broke or wore out, it was probably irreplaceable. By January 1940, food was in such short supply that the basics had to be rationed, and a huge effort was put into producing more food at home, as everything imported from abroad risked the lives of the sailors transporting it.

Just a week after Chamberlain's broadcast, troops of the British Expeditionary Force embarked for France. These were well trained, but poorly equipped, regular and reserve soldiers, later to be joined by conscripts. For those 'back home' the trials of separation and the fear of the loss of their loved ones was the first impact of the war. But they, and the country, were also faced with the practical problem of a loss of manpower at the same time as having to increase production of armaments. This meant that the country had to call on that great, untapped source of labour – women. Eventually, the majority of the female population would be directed into some sort of 'war work'.

Most of the women involved in war work had other duties and responsibilities. As parents, they were often the sole carer, if their husband was called up. Even for men not in the military, home life was difficult. As the war progressed, hours of work lengthened, especially in factories, where most people worked a ten hour day. After work, there were other duties. For women this usually entailed the management of household chores, shopping and food preparation; for men, and some women, shifts in civil defence or voluntary service.

Children's home life was disrupted and disturbed as a consequence of the war. Either they saw less of their parents than before the war or they were evacuated away from them. Evacuation was a precaution to avoid large-scale casualties from aerial bombardment. Children and their mothers, if the children were very young; pregnant women; the frail and the sick were moved from the major population centres to the countryside. Initially, there was little bombing, but one year on from Chamberlain's announcement, Britain saw the beginning of the Blitz. Not for centuries had British civilians been so exposed to physical attack from an enemy.

The images in this book, drawn from the impressive archive of the *Daily Mail*, have been restored to their original condition. They illustrate how Britain itself became the front line and how everyone in the country had a role to play in defending the country and its values.

Everyone's a fighter

As a consequence of the development of aerial warfare the Second World War moved British civilians into the line of fire in a way that, as inhabitants of a powerful island state, they had never dreamed possible. But while bombing brought physical danger, there were other consequences of war. As an island, Britain was better able than other countries on mainland Europe to defend itself – invasion troops would have to land by boat. However, as an island and a sophisticated economic society, dependent on trade by sea to earn revenue and keep it supplied with food, it was vulnerable. Very quickly, the country had to increase home food production and its citizens had to learn to live with rationed food and other essentials, as well as learning how to do without many of the things they had taken for granted before the war.

At the same time as dealing with physical dangers and deprivations, the people of Britain also had to deal with the emotional difficulties engendered by loss, separation and fear. As in all wars, the immediate worry was of the loss of loved ones at the front, but as aerial bombardment brought the war to the heart of Britain, new fears manifested themselves. It was possible to lose those you thought to be safe at home, to lose your home and your community. For many city parents the loss was of their children who were evacuated to the safety of the countryside, away from the danger of the bombing. The children in turn lost, not only their parents, but their way of life. Everyone, in one way or another, lost their way of life.

Men too old to be called up or those in reserved occupations, the jobs that required special skills or expertise, found themselves working longer hours, and for the most part, producing entirely different products. Virtually the entire manufacturing industry of the country converted to weapons production, although some factories, such as Cadbury's Chocolate and Yardley Cosmetics, continued to produce some of their original products as morale boosters. As munitions production increased, other buildings were converted to manufacturing; working conditions in many of these premises were little more than basic. Despite the conditions, workers responded with amazing determination, increasing production so that at some stages shipyards were turning out one ship a week and, following the loss of aircraft at Dunkirk, aircraft factories were able to supply the RAF with the planes they required to fight the Battle of Britain.

The drive to increase production meant the need for a corresponding increase in the workforce. With three-and-a half million men in the forces and those left behind already working long hours on essential war work, the country called on the pool of labour they had last called on during the 1914-1918 war – women. After the Great War, women workers had swiftly been sent back to their traditional roles as homemakers, so that at the outbreak of the Second World War, few were in paid employment.

In January 1940, Winston Churchill, then First Lord of the Admiralty, called for a million women to help with war work, chiefly in the making of munitions. This was the first of many calls to women to help – the classic poster with the slogan 'Women of Britain: Come into the Factories' stems from this period. By the beginning of 1942 the request for volunteers had turned into compulsion and women with no pressing responsibilities in the home were conscripted to do essential war work in the factories or on the land, or to join the forces. Even those with young children or looking after the elderly or the infirm were expected to take on some sort of work to aid the war effort. They worked part-time outside the home if possible or became 'outworkers', making or assembling small machine parts at home.

Despite long hours and compulsory overtime, large numbers of men and women took on extra responsibilities in the Home Guard, the Air Raid Precautionary Service (ARP) or fire watching on the roofs of factories and public buildings, looking out for fires started by incendiary bombs. Charities and religious organisations relied on their members to help support bomb victims: making tea, offering sympathy, managing and staffing rest centres and temporary accommodation for those made homeless by the bombing. There were many important tasks like this to be performed over and above individual work commitments. Breaks from such relentless contribution to the war effort were rare. Factory workers sometimes had to work shifts seven days a week; office workers who took on weekend shifts in factories offered the full-time workers some relief. Holidays were a rarity, although it was possible to take a break on a farm, gaining free accommodation in return for helping with farm work, especially at planting and harvest.

Inevitably, with adults working or volunteering much of their time, children's lives were often strangely free. School, that staple filler of most children's days, was disrupted to varying degrees, depending on where children were. War broke out at the end of the long summer holiday and, initially, the return to school was postponed indefinitely. However, within a few weeks most children were receiving some sort of schooling. In the areas to which evacuees were sent, there were difficulties fitting many more children into small village schools. In cities and towns school buildings suffered damage from bombing or were commandeered to accommodate the homeless and displaced. And, of course, there was a shortage of people to teach them. All this meant that many children did not receive a full-time education for most of the war.

There were reports of vandalism to public shelters and some rowdy behaviour, but for the most part children had enough to do to keep them productively occupied. Some of those activities were clearly dangerous – collecting 'war souvenirs' such as bits of bombs and crashed planes put children at great risk. More legitimate forms of entertainment were radio programmes such as *Children's Hour* and Saturday morning cinema which offered cartoons, short films and serials such as *Tarzan* and *The Lone Ranger*. However, children were also expected to contribute to the war effort. They were frequently the backbone of the many salvage drives run by the Women's Voluntary Service (WVS). These salvage drives collected unused household items and waste, such as pots and pans, rags and paper, which provided some of the raw materials for munitions. The WVS also organised the harvesting of wild fruits and plants such as blackberries, crab apples and mushrooms which were eaten or made into preserves; children provided much of the labour for these harvests. They also collected wild rosehips which were turned into a syrup rich in vitamin C, which was then dispensed to children!

The huge effort that went into collecting food from the wild and the drives to salvage usable materials and waste gives some indication of what made everyone's daily life an immense struggle – the shortage of resources. It was truly a fight for survival day to day. And yet this was not a free-for-all; the government planned and put systems in place to ensure that rich, poor, young and old could share the resources that were available. And the British people, for the most part, behaved with a calm dignity, learning to queue endlessly, learning to 'make do and mend'.

Food rationing began as early as January 1940, starting with butter, sugar and bacon, but extended to include a large number of basic foodstuffs. Everyone was issued with a ration book of coupons entitling them to what nutritionists had calculated was an adequate portion of each rationed item per week. Rationed items could only be bought, at a controlled price, from shops with which you were registered. Fresh foods such as fruit and vegetables, fish and offal were not rationed but were frequently in short supply; it was often necessary to queue for these items, although sometimes the shopkeeper might retain some 'under the counter' for regular customers. This 'under the counter' arrangement was not the same as the 'black market'. On the 'black market' suppliers charged whatever price could be obtained and often the provenance of the goods was questionable.

Luxury items soon disappeared from the shelves as German U-Boats harried shipping around Britain. Only essential items could be imported and materials for munitions took priority. In June 1941, clothes rationing was introduced. The clothes on sale were 'Utility' items, unfussy styles and sometimes rather drab, using a minimum of materials. There were also 'Utility' items in furniture, available only to those who could prove need – newly marrieds or those made homeless by bombing. People got used to reusing and recycling the materials they had: children's clothing could be made by cutting down or restyling worn-out adult clothes; old woollens were unravelled and reknitted; an old drawer fashioned into a baby's cot; shoe polish used to colour stockingless legs! Some items, once worn out or damaged beyond repair, could not be replaced – they were no longer manufactured.

Rationing affected not only food, clothing and household items but fuel, soap and even the amount of water available for baths. Petrol was the first fuel to be rationed. Car ownership was relatively rare and many private cars were immobilised 'for the duration'. Petrol coupons could only be obtained if it could be demonstrated that there was a contribution to the 'war effort' which had a priority call on all fuel; domestic needs were secondary. Thus from quite early on it was the case that everyone was allowed only one bath, no deeper than 5 inches (about 13 cms), per week. The power required to heat that water relied either directly or indirectly on coal, since it was used to produce both gas and electricity; as the war dragged on, coal was

also rationed. Much of this was as a result of a shortage of manpower to dig the coal. Consequently, in December 1943 one in ten of conscripted men were sent to work in the mines – the 'Bevin Boys' as they became known after the minister, Ernest Bevin, who oversaw the scheme.

The economic and emotional costs of the war meant that every man, woman and child in the country had to contribute in huge measure with their energies, savings, possessions and, sometimes, their lives. Partly because Britain, supported by the Commonwealth, had to fight alone for a period of 18 months, it was the case that more than in any previous war, there was a 'Home Front' on which everyone had a part to play: the ARP warden protecting against the effects of aerial bombardment; the worker in the munitions factory working long shifts at production levels unthinkable in peace time; the housewife 'making do and mending'; the volunteers, many of them children, who took part in salvage drives, collecting essential raw materials.

Funding the war meant that when it ended Britain faced years of austerity. Food rationing continued for a further nine years until June 1954. The entire economy had to change from a wartime to a peacetime footing. But more than this, the end of the war meant the task of rebuilding relationships and communities had to be faced. Married couples, parents and children, had often been parted for long stretches of time and some communities had suffered so badly in the bombing that they had disappeared. The whole nation faced the prospect of a long struggle to rebuild itself, both physically and spiritually.

Raiders from the sky

Left: Citizens of London look to the skies for RAF fighters dispatched to meet enemy aircraft during the Battle of Britain. The Luftwaffe's task during the summer of 1940 was to damage the RAF and the means of aircraft production so that invading troop barges could land without being attacked from the air.

Below: A church in Southampton damaged during a raid in October 1940. When the invasion was called off, Germany sought to defeat Britain by bombing the towns and cities in what became known as 'the Blitz'.

Opposite above: Taken in November 1940, this picture was designed to reassure people that the Nazi propaganda suggesting wholesale destruction to London during the Blitz was largely unfounded. Here Ludgate Hill and Fleet Street beyond show no signs of damage.

Opposite below: Winston Churchill, with King George VI and Queen Elizabeth, inspects damage to the rear of Buckingham Palace, caused when two bombs fell on the palace during September 1940.

Londoners carry on

Above: Despite the height of the Blitz in February 1941, Londoners queue for the opening performance of Mozart's *The Marriage of Figaro* at the New Theatre.

Right: In March 1942 a gas alert shows people unconcerned and unprepared for a gas attack. No-one is carrying a gas mask; there were no gas attacks during the war and the distribution of 38 million gas masks, including Mickey Mouse-faced ones for children and complete suits for babies, proved an unnecessary precaution.

Opposite page: Bombing was a two-way process. After the early bombing raids on major towns and cities in Britain during the autumn of 1940, tactical bombing became a weapon of the RAF as well as of the Luftwaffe.

Take a letter, Miss...

Opposite page: After a raid forced them to leave their office, this company's staff, like many others, carried on in the open air, with steel helmets to protect them from flying debris.

Above: The Queen's Messengers Food Convoy distributes hot food and drink to the people of Coventry bombed out of their homes. Much of the help offered to individuals and families affected by the bombing came from churches, charities and organisations such as the Red Cross and the Salvation Army whose expertise the government was pleased to utilise.

Left: A horsebox converted and staffed by Girl Guides provides a mobile canteen to feed members of the Pioneer Corps as they take a break from their duties on demolition work to make safe buildings damaged during bombing raids.

Communal cooking

Above: London County Council set up communal cooking centres for people without gas or other mains services due to the bombing. Food was sold at low cost, but customers had to bring their own dishes and carry it home to eat.

Right: By May 1941 many workers had been bombed out of their homes and their workplaces. Here they queue for soup dispensed from a van provided by the United States. The USA did not join the war until December 1941 but before that time, they helped Britain with many resources, not just food aid. In March 1941 the Lend-Lease Bill had come into effect, allowing the US to lease military equipment, paid for by the US government, to Britain.

Opposite page: A communal feeding centre in south London where even those not made homeless had few places to buy food as many of the shops had been damaged in raids.

Portable Post Office

Above: An experimental new service was tried out in Jewin Street in August 1941. The portable Post Office was designed to be erected in 30 minutes to provide postal facilities to any area of London where the local Post Office was put out of action.

Right: Empty houses in London's West End. It was suggested these be used to house those made homeless in the East End which had suffered badly in the bombing. Some lucky few did find themselves in such accommodation.

Opposite page: Disruption did not just come with damage to buildings. Unexploded bombs caused the temporary evacuation of premises. Here a caller to the newspaper offices housed in this London street is redirected.

Traffic problems

Right: Motorists flocked to the AA and RAC in October 1940 to register with the 'Help your neighbour' scheme, an attempt to give lifts to workers finding it difficult to get to work. Registered motorists were given extra petrol coupons. Petrol was rationed in the first month of the war - a necessity, given Britain had to import all its oil.

Below: As petrol became harder to obtain, motorists tried new sources of fuel - here is a gas powered car.

Opposite above: Piccadilly in early January 1940, once one of London's busiest streets, shows few mobile private cars; a new 25-shilling car tax had come into effect at the beginning of the month as part of a scheme to discourage car use. Many motorists decommissioned their cars for the duration, not forgetting to immobilise them by removing the rotor arm, in case they provided transport for enemy invaders!

Opposite below: While many wait at the bus stop, this gentleman gets around on his bicycle.

Chauffeur-driven tandem

Right: The fact that he is unable to obtain petrol for his car does not stop this City gent from being chauffeur-driven to work.

Above: The midget car which could do eighty miles to the gallon proves an attraction on this London street and a fine way to make the petrol ration last.

Opposite page: Apart from the fact that they are travelling to work on a tandem and have to carry gas masks, everything seems normal for these two men as they set off for work: one with his bowler hat, umbrella and a kiss for the wife; the other reads the paper while waiting.

On the buses

Opposite above: Buses were an important means of transport throughout the war. Here workmen change the seating plan of a bus to enable it to carry a further twenty to thirty standing passengers.

Opposite below: Joan Chapman, a London bus conductress, was responsible for the 'Billy Brown' slogans which gave passengers directions in rhyme. She is pictured here with one of her slogans.

Above: As shortages grew, every aspect of life had to cope. In July 1942 London buses which would have returned to their depots after the morning rush hour were parked up in central London for the day. This saved both petrol and tyre rubber.

Right: A strike on the London bus service in 1944 meant that the army were called in to keep the buses on the road.

Hogmanay trains

Right: A scramble for seats on a train to Scotland on 31 December 1943. Extra trains were run for the many troops going on leave for the New Year.

Opposite above: Just weeks before the D Day landings there is a restricted train service for civilians who have to wait until all the military are on board.

Opposite below: At the beginning of June 1944 an ammunition train blew up near Soham in Cambridgeshire. At this time thousands of tons of munitions were being transported around the country in preparation for the D Day invasion of Europe.

Above: An army lorry transports people during the 1944 bus strike.

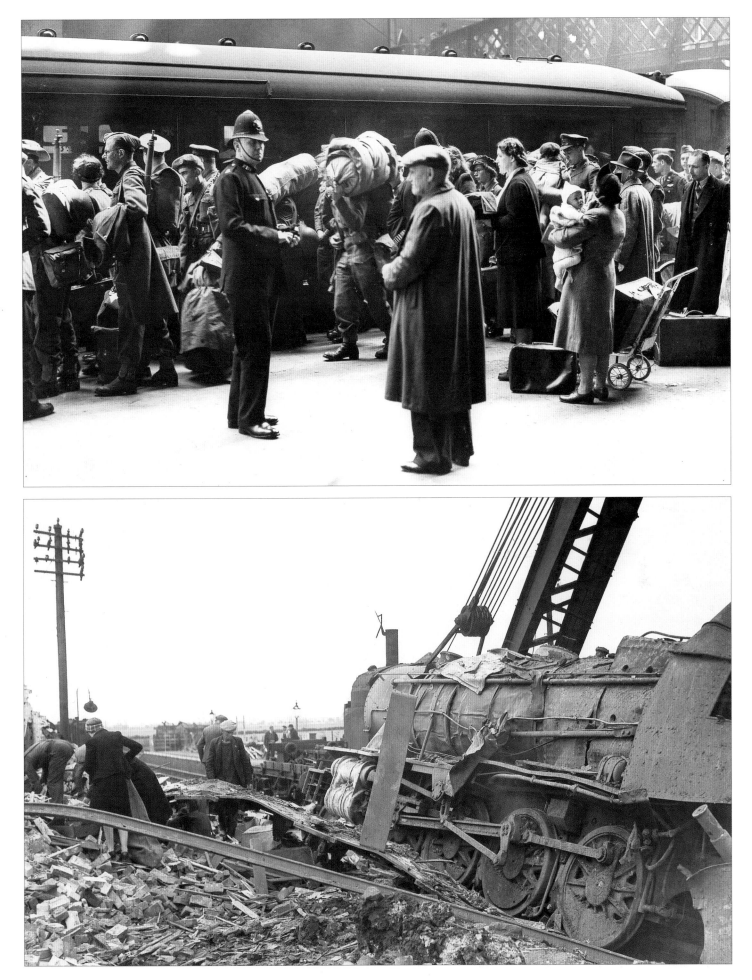

Salvage

Above left: Servants from the Lord Mayor's Mansion House add to the fifty-six million books collected as part of a public appeal for books to be donated for pulping or reuse.

Above right: Boy Scouts in Cardiff collect waste paper. With the fall of Norway in May 1940, a main source of wood pulp for paper was cut off, making it essential to collect waste paper – over a millions tons were collected over the course of four years.

Left: The principal use for waste paper was in the manufacture of munitions.

Opposite page: A mountain of waste paper awaits pulping. Paper was not to be used for any unnecessary wrapping of products and toilet paper was in short supply.

WASTE PAPER GOES TO WAR

Manchester metal

Above: A workman in Manchester takes a sledge hammer to the ornamental ironwork on one of the city's lamp posts. The iron would be resmelted and used in the manufacture of munitions.

Left: The railings surrounding the play area of the Princesses Elizabeth and Margaret go to the salvage drive.

Opposite above: Children in Croydon who brought in waste paper were given a pony ride as a reward. The drive to salvage materials was backed by persuasive poster techniques. It paid off and by 1943 each household in the country had donated, on average, about half a ton of salvage.

Opposite below: A dump of salvaged rubber tyres waits to be recycled.

Any old iron?

A resident of Acton contributes to the first 'Scrap Week' in February 1940. Metal was an obvious requirement for the making of munitions. The British public donated nearly one-and-a-half million tons, enough to build 50,000 tanks.

Opposite above: Berkeley Square, built in 1709, loses its historic railings to the drive for salvage.

Opposite below: Ornamental railings and gates are removed from residential properties owned by the L. M. S. Railway.

Can bank

Opposite page: A workman shovels some of the huge bank of cans collected by East Ham Borough Corporation whose residents donated twenty tons each week.

Right: While it may look like these men are carrying ladders, they are in fact transporting railings removed from a local park in Hammersmith as part of 'railings week'. The railings were presented to the nation to be used for armaments. Private owners of railings were persuaded to do likewise. The collection of metal from such salvage schemes is estimated to have saved around 400 merchant ships and the lives of thousands of sailors.

Below: Donated pots and pans at an aluminium reception centre where the metal was gathered for re-use in the aircraft industry.

Ration books

Left: Ration books are prepared by clerks at the Food Executive Office. Although the individual coupons, each slightly smaller than the size of a postage stamp, were printed, the owner's details on each book had to be filled out by hand. Food rationing began in January 1940, originally with bacon, butter and sugar, but expanded to cover all processed food, as well as meat, eggs and milk.

Above: The shop window looks reasonably well-stocked two months into war, but going about the business of shopping is decidedly different. Entry to the shop is over a line of protective sandbags.

Opposite above: Queuing in the rain for fish on Good Friday 1943. Fish was 'off the ration' but was often in short supply - there were shortages of fishermen and increased dangers in putting out to sea during wartime.

Opposite below: Window shopping during the first weeks of the Blitz. The milliner's shop has products to display but has had to protect the plate glass frontage from bomb damage.

The perfect seam

Opposite page: Silk or nylon stockings were in extremely short supply by the summer of 1942, despite the presence of American GIs in Britain who could sometimes get hold of stockings from the US. Most women had to find ingenious methods of dressing their legs. Favourites were rubbing gravy browning or shoe polish mixed with cream on to the legs, or just leaving the legs natural and pencilling, or painting, on a seam to give the illusion of stockings. The device here was designed by Max Factor and was intended to enable the user to draw a perfect seam.

Left: Petticoat Lane Market in June 1941 just after the introduction of clothing coupons. These had to be used to purchase new clothes which were now rationed; second-hand clothes could be bought and sold without coupons.

Below: Clothing coupons change hands in this street market.

Suits you, sir!

Left: Anti-aircraft gunner Philip Fogel, a clothes designer before the war, created this suit which was to cost only two pounds. He hoped to interest some major firms in his prototype which, although the model photographed here was made for a six-foot-tall Guardsman, used a minimum of fabric.

Above: 'Utility' designs were intended to provide stylish clothing but using a minimum of materials: men's trousers had no turn-ups; jackets were single breasted; skirt and jacket lengths were shorter than before the war; there were fewer buttons on the front, no cuff buttons; and no fussy details or frills were included.

Opposite above and below: On 26 July 1942 sweets became subject to rationing. These people are queuing outside shops in the Strand (*above*) and Leicester Square (*below*) to buy sweets the day rationing started. The sweet ration ranged from two to four ounces per person per week, the equivalent of a Mars bar.

Coal shortages

Opposite above: A coal shortage in southern England at the beginning of 1945 saw the populace having to be creative. These people have collected fuel from the nearby wood.

Opposite below right: Sifting the cinders to see if there is anything to be reused.

Opposite below left: Soldiers delivering coal after the end of the war. The demobilisation of troops took a long time and in the meantime they helped the country get back to normal.

Above: Marylebone Council store coal at this bomb site in Baker Street to avoid congestion on the rail network at peak times.

Left: Queuing for fresh cherries in June 1945. Despite the end of the war in Europe, things were far from getting back to normal and some shortages got worse.

There's a queue for everything

Right: Queuing for woollens knitted by the women of Australia. The customers still had to surrender clothing coupons for each item.

Below: Women wait patiently for their turn to buy vegetables from a street stall.

Opposite above: An orderly queue for potatoes. Fresh fruit and vegetables were not rationed but it was sometimes difficult, often because of transportation problems, to keep shops supplied.

Opposite below: Rumours that the owner of this stall would have fish for sale caused a queue to form hours before it arrived.

Lend a hand on the land

Left: A march through West Drayton for the Women's Allotment Week. One way of increasing a family's food supply was to 'grow your own'. Private gardens were pressed into service and a large proportion of public space in parks, school grounds and sports pitches was given over to allotments.

Below: Soldiers from anti-aircraft batteries help ready the ground in a London park in preparation for allotments. This was all part of the 'grow more food' campaign started at the beginning of 1940 to coincide with the introduction of food rationing.

Opposite page: Redcross Street Fire Station firefighters cultivated these productive and neatly kept allotments amid the ruins of the City.

Dig for Victory

Opposite page: Fighter pilots, in full flying kit, put in a spot of digging during a lull in activity. Air crews did have quite a bit of down time as they waited for the next mission and cultivating vegetables to supplement the mess rations was a useful way of spending the time.

Above: These men and women digging on allotments in London's Victoria Park were just some of the hundreds of people around the country out working on the land on 'Dig for Victory Sunday' in March 1940. By 1943 there were nearly one and a half million allotments in Britain, tended by millions of men, women and children in their 'spare' time.

Right: Eton schoolboys off to the school's allotments to 'do their bit' for the war effort.

We want to be WAAFs

Opposite above: A queue of women outside Aeriel House in the Strand following an appeal on the BBC in the second week of the war for more members of the Women's Auxiliary Air Force (WAAF).

Opposite below: WAAFs wave from the back of a lorry during training.

Left: Breakfast in the mess before the WAAF's duties which might include cooking for the RAF, clerical work or cleaning and preparing equipment.

Below: This WAAF is cutting out a fabric patch to be used to repair a barrage balloon. Barrage balloons were essential defensive equipment which were raised when an enemy attack was signalled. The balloons and the cables that tethered them were obstacles to low-flying aircraft, preventing clear bomb targeting.

Women design planes

Opposite below: A group of women training to make the thousands of drawings needed for the construction of aircraft. The woman overseeing their work is Mrs 'Blossom' Miles, Britain's first female aircraft designer and wife of the factory owner.

Opposite above: Women from the Auxiliary Territorial Service (ATS) collect spent shells from the sands after firing tests. Initially, it was intended that women should have no military duties but it soon became clear that the ATS women in anti-aircraft batteries were vital to civil defence.

Left: A WAAF from a London barrage balloon unit is shown how to adjust her new greatcoat, essential wear in the winter nights during the 1940 Blitz.

Above: Concentration on the face of this WAAF during an officer training session.

Women make planes

Right: Women packing a Hercules engine ready for dispatch. From early on in the war, women were called upon to take up work in the aircraft and munitions industries.

Below: At the College of Aeronautical Engineering in Wimbledon, these women learn to be aircraft inspectors.

Opposite above: Monitoring output in the control room of one of the Ministry of Aircraft Production's underground factories.

Opposite below: 'In the crankcase assembly shop, girl operatives have mastered the intricate work which was previously only touched by the masculine hand.' Thus reads the original caption to this picture of a woman working on a Rolls-Royce Merlin engine.

Free showers

Opposite page: Lambeth's mobile decontamination van, for use in the event of bombing disturbing dangerous substances, being demonstrated in the street and providing a free shower for the neighbourhood children.

Right: As invasion fears grew following the withdrawal from Dunkirk, local authorities on the south coast tried to prevent an exodus of people from the area. Here Brian Crozier Williams, a member of the town of Worthing's Chamber of Trade fixes a sticker to a car, encouraging people to 'stay put'.

Below left: Girls at work in Buxton Street School, Whitechapel in March 1940. From the beginning of the month it became compulsory for all children aged 11 and over to attend school, at least part-time.

Below right: The boys of Malvern School, evacuated to Blenheim Palace for safety, read in their new dormitory in the Long Gallery.

Childhood memories

Above: War or no war, these children will remember the conjuror's performance in Wilmington Square, London on Whit Bank Holiday 1942.

Left: An Etonian who will probably remember the first Long Leave of the war, during which the boys had to stay at school owing to transport difficulties. He's one of the lucky ones whose relatives managed to come to visit.

Opposite above: Girls from Roedean School walk through the streets of Keswick, the town to which the school was evacuated.

Opposite below left: Boys at Eton are given permission not to wear their top hats as it could hamper the quick fitting on of gas masks. They were also given permission not to carry their gas masks with them in school.

Opposite below right: Christmas 1942 and a couple of secondary school children help deliver the Christmas mail.

The boys to entertain you

Opposite above: A band from a New Zealand infantry brigade plays a lunchtime concert outside the Royal Exchange. The banner promoting War Bonds is a reminder that ordinary citizens helped finance the war by investing in bonds which were to be repaid, with interest, once hostilities ceased.

Opposite below: The Life Guards play at a concert in St James's Park in April 1945, possibly a prelude to their part in the Victory Parade the following month.

Above and right: American soldiers and British WAAFs at a Whit Bank Holiday fair in Hampstead in 1942. The Americans had entered the war after the attack on Pearl Harbor in 1941 and the first American soldiers had landed in Britain in January 1942. They were known as GIs, an abbreviation of 'General Issue' which referred to their uniform and kit.

A nice cup of tea

Left: This soldier, burdened with two rifles and his kit, is glad of a refreshing cup of tea as he waits at a London railway station for a delayed train.

Opposite above: A WAAF, out on the town, is checked up on by WAAF Military Police. All the services had their own police who ensured that those away from barracks had the required passes and that they behaved themselves!

Opposite below: Two soldiers are given a cup of tea from a canteen set up at a London station to supply meals for the troops passing through.

Love is in the air

Above: A Canadian soldier and his girlfriend among the first signs of spring: crocuses in a London park.

Right: Private George Pinnock, on a 72-hour pass from his regiment, marries Miss Joan Cox in April 1940. The couple were to see each other just once in the next five years.

Far right: He's home on leave and they have time to feed the pigeons in Trafalgar Square.

Opposite page: An American sailor and a British ATS girl hold hands while listening at Speakers' Corner by London's Hyde Park.

GI brides

Above: The bride and her American GI groom leave their marriage ceremony in style. Eighty thousand British women married American soldiers during the war and became known as 'GI brides'.

Right: GI brides and their babies get ready to fly to America for Christmas 1946. Unfortunately, their flight was turned back because of bad weather. These women and their children had to wait for another opportunity to reach their new home.

Opposite: Taken during the first two weeks of the war, this couple are probably saying their farewells before he leaves for France with the British Expeditionary Force (BEF).

Soldiers' recreation

Left: 'Who would not be a soldier?' questions the caption to this photograph taken of soldiers during a break from basic training in August 1940.

Below: Canadian soldiers play a game of volleyball, a game never seen in Britain before the war.

Opposite above: Not quite recreation! These searchlight operators are playing a game with aircraft recognition cards.

Opposite below: August Bank Holiday 1940, and the line of spectators at Derbyshire's Bakewell cricket ground are troops from a nearby barracks.

Crowds gather

Opposite above: People gather in Whitehall to see the 'comings and goings' at government offices. In an era without twenty-four-hour news, people often felt the need to be close to unfolding events. Apart from newspapers, the BBC's Home Service was the only source for the dissemination of news, its television service to 20,000 pre-war viewers having been suspended.

Opposite below left: Crowds gather outside Downing Street as Norway and Denmark are subject to a German blitzkrieg in April 1940.

Opposite below right: Serious faces in Downing Street as the fall of France seems imminent.

Right: The British Museum Reading Room re-opens two weeks after the start of the war.

Below left: The City on 5 September 1939 when the Stock Exchange remained closed.

Below right: Foreign Secretary, Lord Halifax and Sir Alexander Cadogan, carrying their gas masks, are part of the 'comings and goings' in Whitehall.

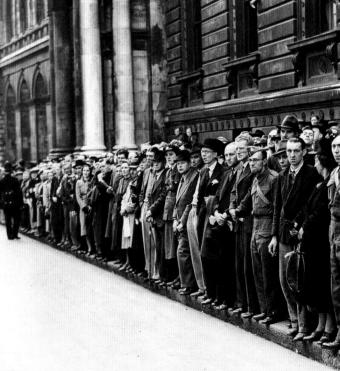

Changing sights

Left and below: September 1939 and a change to the Changing of the Guard ceremony at Buckingham Palace. Instead of traditional uniforms, the guards wear khaki and steel helmets.

Opposite above: Guards marching through Piccadilly becomes a common sight for Londoners as Christmas 1939 approaches.

Opposite below left: Pictured on the day war was declared, the caption accompanying this picture reads: 'Standing firm, as the rest of Britain is standing firm, this sentry typifies the spirit of this country today.'

Opposite below right: Winston Churchill inspects the Parliamentary Home Guard.

'Der Tag'

Above left and right: 'Today was "Der Tag" day but Hitler only arrived at Buckingham Palace in the form of an effigy, which was hung on a tree in the Green Park.' The original caption to these photographs refers to the fact that 15 August 1940 was one of the dates speculated as being the day the Germans would invade Britain. However, the victory of the RAF over the Luftwaffe in the Battle of Britain meant that Germany could not offer cover for landing troops and the invasion was cancelled.

Right: This crowd is unperturbed by 'Der Tag' as they queue for the cinema.

Opposite above: Winston Churchill, in his 'siren suit' broadcasts to the nation in June 1942.

Opposite below left: In June 1943, Churchill speaks to an audience at the Guildhall about the necessity of a German unconditional surrender.

Opposite below right: Churchill salutes on his return from a review of the troops in the Middle East in February 1943.

Animal casualties

Opposite above: Animal lovers queue outside the Animal Defence League in City Road, London. Rather than leave the animals to fend for themselves when their owners were evacuated the animals were destroyed. In London alone, 40,000 animals were humanely gassed in the first few days of the war. London Zoo also destroyed animals such as poisonous snakes or other creatures that could be a danger to the public if they escaped during a raid.

Opposite below: Some lucky animals evacuated by the RSPCA to safe billets in the country.

Above: An 'unofficial' two minutes' silence at the Cenotaph on 11 November 1940.

Left: Petticoat Lane Sunday Market closes for a National Day of Prayer as the evacuation of troops from Dunkirk begins on 26 May 1940.

Eros taken to safety

Above left: The statue of Eros was removed from its pedestal in Piccadilly Circus and evacuated to safety for the duration of the war. Here, in October 1939, scaffolding is being erected to enable removal.

Above right: Like many public monuments, the pedestal on which Eros stood and the fountain below it was sandbagged to protect it during bombing raids.

Right: The statue of King Charles I in Trafalgar Square is covered with corrugated iron to protect it from damage during air raids.

Opposite page: At the beginning of July 1941, workmen tie the equestrian statue of King Charles I to a lorry in preparation for its removal to 'a safe country retreat'. After the Blitz it was moved to a safer location in the country as it was judged too much of a risk to leave it in the square.

Under wraps for the duration

Above and left: A 'Christmas Treat Fund' poster is erected over the sandbagged fountain and plinth for the Eros statue which, like the 300,000 London children the fund aimed to help, had been evacuated to safety in the country. It was the first Christmas of the war and for many children, and their parents, it was a difficult one for those who could not be together as a family.

Opposite above: An attempt to cover up the ugly sandbagged facade of the Eros fountain with a life size frieze depicting some typical scenes from Piccadilly Circus. The project was part of the War Savings Campaign to persuade citizens to donate their savings to the war effort.

Opposite below: A relatively unusual sight during the war as tanks passed round Marble Arch in May 1940. The tanks were travelling between bases but it was not normal practice for them to take a route through central London.

Civilians relax

Below: In the shadow of a barrage balloon in a London park, a quiet game of bowls progresses.

Right: Two women relax as they sit inside the empty fountain basin in Trafalgar Square listening to a lunchtime concert given by the Grenadier Guards.

Opposite above: The Royal Artillery Memorial at Hyde Park Corner is surrounded by weeds as neither the time nor the labour can be spared to keep the weeds down.

Opposite below: A sand dump at Hyde Park Corner, usually the most carefully tended of thoroughfares, is left to grow wild.

Wartime humour

Opposite right above: At the height of the Blitz a pub landlord repairs the windows of his saloon and adds his own touch of humour to the boards.

Opposite right below: The 'Blue Book', a government publication which detailed pre-war diplomatic communications, is on sale at this stall; the cover of the book was white!

Opposite left: Humorously billed as the first casualty of the war, Gunner Gibson had his foot crushed by a tractor soon after the declaration of war.

Above: The shortage of newsprint provoked the caption to this photograph: 'Share your *Daily Mail*.'

Right: Couples enjoy free dancing in Regent's Park at Whitsun 1942.

Keep smiling through

Left: Although life was difficult with shortages, long work hours, dangers and worries, people seized as many opportunities as possible to enjoy themselves. A woman 'tests her strength' at the Fair on Hampstead Heath, Easter 1943.

Above: Easter Monday 1941 in London's New Coventry Street and holiday-makers crowd the streets. 'Restaurants and cinemas did good business.'

Opposite above: An open-air dance in Brockwell Park. Dances were very popular and took place anywhere from a village hall to a park. The music was always live, quite often supplied by military bands.

Opposite below: Queuing for boats on the Serpentine on a warm May day in 1941.

Chins up

Despite petrol rationing a big crowd turned up for the 1941
Derby. Most sports were suspended or ran a limited programme
for the duration of the war. Football reorganised into Northern
and Southern leagues, but as most of the players were in the
Services it was difficult to maintain regular teams.

Opposite above: 'All the fun of the fair' at Hampstead Heath,
August 1943.

Opposite below: Instead of a trellis work of tape on the windows
to prevent flying glass in the event of bomb damage, this
shopkeeper chose to write an encouraging message.

Victory!

Opposite page: Thousands of people gathered on the steps of St Paul's Cathedral to hear a Salute of Bells to celebrate the liberation of Paris on 25 August 1944. It had taken nearly twelve weeks for the Allies to push through France from the landings in Normandy in June.

Right: News reaches London that Hitler is dead, having committed suicide on 30 April 1945.

Below: News of Germany's final surrender is chalked up on a board in a London club. Others heard the news on their radios and cinemas flashed the information across the screens.

8 May 1940 was designated Victory in Europe (VE) Day and was the cause of huge celebrations. However, it was not the end of the war. The Allies were still fighting the Japanese in the Far East and that war was to continue for another three months. It was not until 15 August 1945, just three weeks short of six years, that the war was finally over for the people of Britain and they could begin working hard at getting back to normal.

The peace

Right: On 17 September 1944 the Blackout ended. It was replaced by the 'Dimout' which allowed slightly brighter street lights and permitted normal curtains to be used at windows; by this time the risk of an air raid and thus the possibility of bombers being guided by lights from the ground was minimal. However, while towns around the country stepped up their lighting a little, London's West End erected its pre-war globes and lamps, ready for victory and the return to normal lighting.

Below: A picture of the emergency bridge across the Thames at Millbank. It was one of three, the others being at Westminster and Battersea, which were built as an insurance in case the permanent bridges were damaged by bombs. None of the temporary bridges ever needed to be used for traffic and after the war they were taken down.

Opposite page: The people of the village of Oreston in Devon turned out to welcome home Sergeant F. G. Tucker who had returned from a German prison camp. With him are his wife and young son. For the Tuckers, like the rest of the population, it was the beginning of readjustment to a life without war imposing on their everyday lives.

ACKNOWLEDGEMENTS

The photographs in this book are from the archives of the *Daily Mail*.
Particular thanks to Steve Torrington, Dave Sheppard, Brian Jackson,
Alan Pinnock, Paul Rossiter, Richard Jones and all the staff.

Thanks also to Cliff Salter, Kate Truman, John Dunne,
Peter Wright, Trevor Bunting, Simon Taylor and Don Henry.

Design by Judy Linard